zen

meditations

on being a mother

roni jay

zen
meditations
on being a mother

SOURCEBOOKS, INC.®
NAPERVILLE, ILLINOIS

Being a mother is one of the most rewarding—and demanding—jobs you can ever be called upon to perform.

At times it may feel as if you are being pulled in a hundred different directions at once, and that there are simply too few hours in the day to accomplish all the chores that must be done. Motherhood is a job like no other, and the rewards of watching your children grow toward independence and confidence are immense—and yet it is all too easy in the rush and bustle of the working day to concentrate on meeting all those different demands of childcare, work, and home without ever stopping for a moment to catch your breath, and consider the real value of the job you are doing.

This book of meditations is designed to help you take a few moments of quiet contemplation to consider the importance of your job as a nurturer, carer, friend, and teacher. Each meditation focuses on a different aspect of motherhood—from coping with temper, to learning to take time to listen—simple issues that are often taken for granted in the daily bustle. Spend as much, or as little, time as you like on each meditation, obviously some will be more relevant to you than others. To help you to achieve the atmosphere of calm contemplation necessary to get the most out of these meditations we have enclosed a CD of soothing music which has been specifically composed to help you relax and focus your mind. As little as half an hour spent quietly contemplating the thoughts and themes of this little book will leave you feeling refreshed and renewed, and more able to cope with the demands—and the joys—of motherhood.

If you throw stones at a jagged rock, it becomes more pitted. If you pour water on it, the rock will eventually become smooth. We often respond to our child's temper by becoming irritated with them. It's a strange way to teach them to control their emotions, by losing control of ours—like trying to calm a stormy sea by throwing water at it. If we really want them to grow into adults who can handle tiredness and frustration, we need to show them by our own example how to do it.

coping with temper

expectation

If you plant a sapling, you wouldn't hope to predict which way all its branches would grow over the years. The more expectations we have for our children, the more we are setting ourselves up for disappointment. They will never want to put out branches in the direction we would choose for them—if we could. If we love our children unconditionally, what could we want them to be that is more perfect than what they already are? If they shared our ambitions and interests exactly, they would not be themselves but only copies of us.

magic

Henry Ford said, "Whether you believe you can, or whether you believe you can't, you're absolutely right." The ability to believe in the improbable is a talent for life. If we don't believe in magic when we are children, we have no hope of believing in it as adults. One of the greatest gifts a mother can give her children is a sense of magic and wonder, so that their imagination can blossom. Any opportunity to create magic for a child is an opportunity to give that child a truly valuable gift.

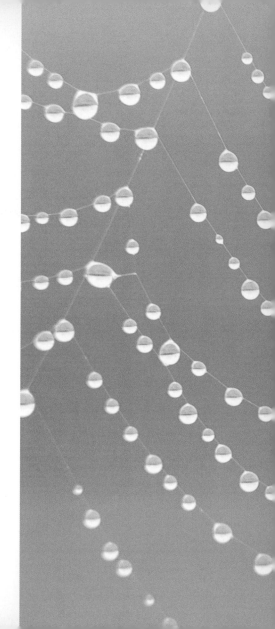

"Whether you believe
you can, or whether you
believe you can't, you're
absolutely right."

living in
the moment

As a green shoot reaches toward the sun, so a child's natural instinct is to look forward, to steer toward adulthood, to learn to be like us. Children are born to reach for the sun. It is easy to join in with them and to think ahead to what they will be when they are older. Then one day we realize that we desperately miss them being younger; the small child we once knew has all but disappeared inside a larger person. Once our children acquire new talents, they will have them for life. But as they grow toward the sun, we can no longer find that first small shoot.

patience

Until we can teach ourselves the simple patience our fellow creatures have, how can we teach our children anything?

Plants, animals, even seeds have patience in abundance—to wait for the spring, to migrate thousands of miles, to teach their young to hunt. We often believe we are the most sophisticated of all creatures, and yet we sometimes lack this basic skill. The times our children make us frustrated or angry are usually the times when they most need us. We are irritated by some lack of ability or understanding on their part, when we should welcome the opportunity to help them learn.

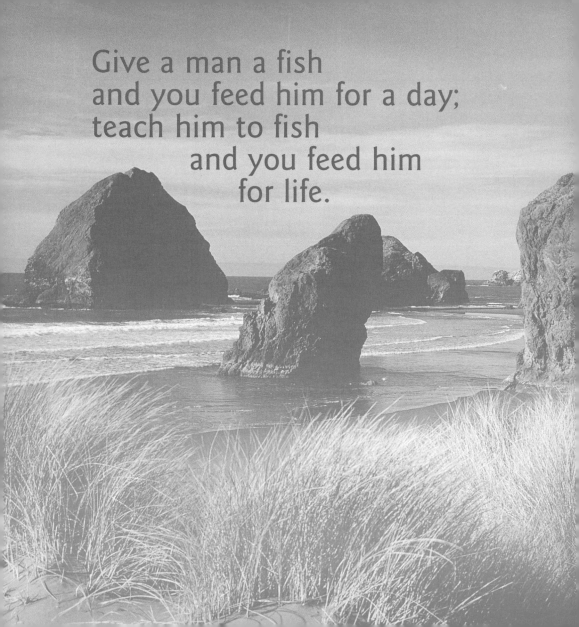

Give a man a fish
and you feed him for a day;
teach him to fish
and you feed him
for life.

teaching

It is our job to teach our children the skills they need for life, but when we simply tell them what to do, we are teaching them nothing. We need to show them, to guide them while they copy us, to let them learn for themselves. Rather than feed our children information, we need to show them how to acquire knowledge for themselves. Then we feed them for life.

learning

We are never so perfect that we have
nothing left to learn, and often our children
are the best teachers. If we want them to
learn from us, how much more equal and
beneficial a relationship if we also learn
from them. If we look, we can see
numerous skills in our children that we lack
—perhaps they have a greater ability to live
for the moment, maybe they can make
decisions intuitively, perhaps they let their
bad temper blow over quickly and they are
all smiles again. When we recognize that
our children have skills we lack, it changes
our relationship with them for the better.

tears When a ewe hears her baby lamb bleat, she searches until she finds it. When a newborn kitten mews, its mother does her best to pacify it. We share the same instinct to soothe and calm our children, and yet we sometimes knowingly cause the tears.

In order to teach our child to behave well, we give them a reprimand, send them to their room, or confiscate the object that poses a danger. We believe it is necessary to do it, and we are generally right, but we can still acknowledge the conflicting instinct to hold our child and soothe away their tears.

two parents

Those who try to do too much achieve less than those who recognize their own limits. Children have two parents because they need two parents. One person alone cannot be everything a child needs. We hope we can all do the absolute basics—providing love and security—but we cannot provide everything else. Some of us are better than others at being gentle, exciting, physically stimulating, intellectually stimulating, cuddly, firm, patient, and all the other things a child needs in a parent. It is not our job to be all these things ourselves—we are bound to fail. It is our job only to ensure that our child has access to these attributes from somewhere.

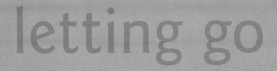

letting go

When an animal breaks free of a trap, it bolts from it never to return. But if we set no trap and simply put out food for it, it will visit every day. If we try to hold on to our children, they will break away from us. But if we allow them to leave at their own speed they will feel safe in returning, knowing that there is no net to snare them.

debt

Our children did not
ask to be born, and
they owe us nothing.

We chose to bring them into
the world, and it is our job to
make sure that they do not
regret our decision. Happiness,
security, and love are our debt
to them. When we provide
these, we have not earned their
gratitude, we have simply
squared the deal.

When a young stag starts to grow into his prime, the old stag knows his position is under threat. When a new baby is on the way, its older brothers or sisters know that their position too is threatened. A mother's job is to make every child feel as precious and as special as if it were the only one. Two stags cannot rule the same herd, but two children can share the same mother. It is not easy, but we find a way because we know we must.

new baby

The sea does not own the fish within it, nor does the oak tree own the saplings that grow around it.

Our children are not ours; we merely have custody of them until they are fully grown. They belong not to us but to themselves. We would insult them if we tried to make them mere images of ourselves. We do not have the right to tell them what they must think or what opinions they should hold. We can only tell them the facts, voice our own opinions, and leave them to make up their own minds.

make believe

A small child cannot tell the difference between reality and make believe much of the time. Many parents try to teach them this difference as early as possible. But there is no need—the brain learns to distinguish in time, no matter what we do. And, once learnt, they will never again be able to blur the boundary. But it is in the blurred divide between reality and fantasy where magic lives. This is the land of Father Christmas and fairies, magic spells and Peter Pan. Would we not serve our children better if we helped them to inhabit this charmed world for as long as possible?

distant future

As we look at our child's sleeping face, or watch it engrossed in play, we wonder and guess at what it will be like years hence. What will it be like when we are not here to see? When it is gray and old, with children of its own perhaps, or even grandchildren? Sometimes we even wonder about our child's death when the time comes. But when the time comes it will not be this little child, but an old, tired, gray soul who passes into death. So long as we help mold an adult who is able to be happy and to fulfill ambitions, that old, gray soul will be ready to go when it is time.

foundation

If you take the last few years from a long life, you have taken nothing else. But if you take away the first few years, you have deprived the whole life.

There is no greater gift we can give our children than their childhood. A happy, secure, and stimulating childhood is worth more than all the money in the world; it is the key that will unlock happiness and fulfillment throughout their life.

greater
love

The swan mates for life. Its cygnets grow into swans and move on to new territories, but its mate stays by its side. Our children will grow and move on, but our partner will remain with us. And it is because our partner is the most important person to us that our children feel free to move on, and create their own family. If we show our children that our partner comes first, we do them a great favor—we give them their freedom.

Without water, the plants cannot grow. Without air, animals cannot survive. Without food, nothing lives. But it is as important to feed the mind as the body, and our children are only half alive if we feed their bodies but not their minds. Mental stimulation is essential; they need new experiences. We can take them to their first football match, borrow new books from the library, take them abroad on holiday, give them a pet rabbit. It doesn't matter what we do, so long as they have variety and newness in their lives. These are the water, air, and food that their minds need to grow and flourish.

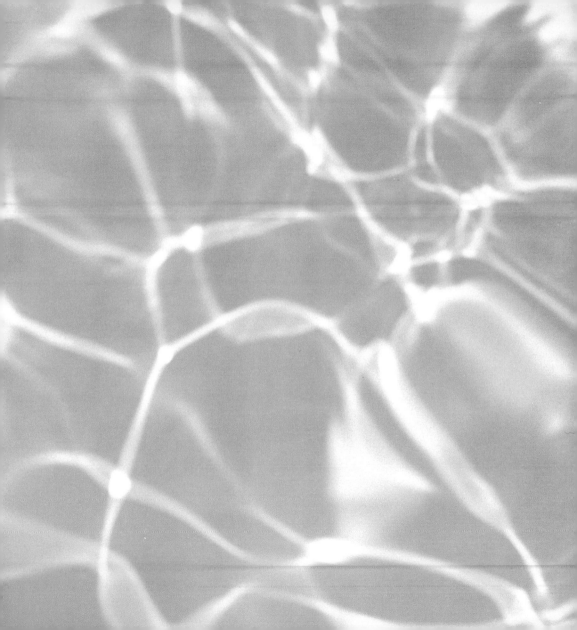

attention

When we want a plant to grow in the garden, it is not enough simply to look at it each day waiting for it to grow. We must plant it in the right spot, weed around it, feed and water it, prune it, and tend it. And when we want our children to develop into healthy specimens, we need to pay them just such attention. They need time devoted to them for reading, chatting, playing together, or simply cuddling. Merely being in the same room is not enough.

looking ahead

What will our child be
when it grows up?
Wondering about our
child's future career is fun
and exciting. We cannot
know, or direct, or choose.
We can only sit back and
watch, an interested
spectator. They make the
choices, they make all the
decisions. But if we have
done our job well as a
mother, they will make
a wise choice when the
time comes.

mix and match

As we travel through life, we meet many people and interact with them in many different ways.

We can prepare our children for this from an early age by adapting their relationships with the rest of the family. We can spend time with them alone and with our partner. If we have more than one child, we can spend time with just one, or just two of them. Each time we change the group, we change the dynamics. The second child becomes the oldest when their older sibling is absent. The youngest can have time alone with one parent or the other. These simple changes for an hour or two within the family are a preparation for the less secure relationships of later life.

mistakes

We do not learn from other people's mistakes,
only from our own. It is painful as a
mother to watch our child
making mistakes, especially
those we made ourselves.
We want to tell them
to listen to us, to do
it our way. But we can
do no more than offer
advice, and then leave
them to make the
mistake if they must.
And when we were their age, did we always
listen to our own mother?

generations

When we give our child the best childhood we can, we give more than we may know.

We also teach them how to be a good parent, so that they may pass it on to their own children. Just as we learned from our own parents, so will they, and the gift of a happy childhood can be passed down the generations. It is the most valuable gift that we can give to our own flesh and blood who we may never meet— our great-grandchildren and beyond.

Each bird is different. One feeds on seeds, another on worms. One prefers bread, and the next eats insects. If we feed them, we offer a choice of nuts, seeds, and scraps to suit them all.

difference

Our children are all different, too, so surely we should treat them in a variety of ways according to their needs. The rules may be consistent, but we can enforce them according to the child. Some children find it truly hard to be good, some are deeply hurt by the mildest chastisement, some are thick-skinned. By treating them individually, we acknowledge their uniqueness and reinforce their sense of identity.

Books are the door to both knowledge and fantasy for a child.

By reading to them we teach them both to learn and to enjoy. And more than this: the act of reading to them—beside one another on the bed, or snuggled on a lap in front of the fire—creates a whole world of warmth and security, populated by the characters in the story, and with the child at the center of our focus. What more could a child ask?

reading

redundancy

A mother cat feeds her kittens when they are newborn, but she soon teaches them to hunt for themselves. It is the role of a mother to prepare her children from the start for life without her.

If our children still need us once they reach adulthood, we have not done our job well. It is our aim to make ourselves redundant. We hope our children will continue to want us and to value us, but they should not need us. So whenever we hear, "Leave me alone, I can do it myself," we should congratulate ourselves.

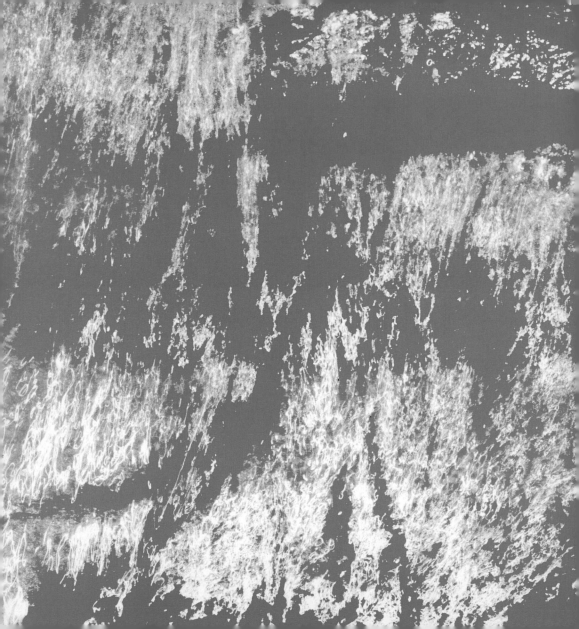

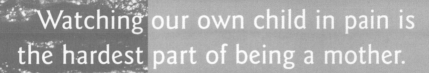

Watching our own child in pain is the hardest part of being a mother.

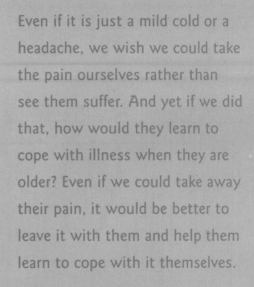

Even if it is just a mild cold or a headache, we wish we could take the pain ourselves rather than see them suffer. And yet if we did that, how would they learn to cope with illness when they are older? Even if we could take away their pain, it would be better to leave it with them and help them learn to cope with it themselves.

illness

school

When a man crosses a mountain, he finds a new land on the other side.

And when children make the transition to school, they enter a new world. A world so different that they often take on a whole new persona once they are there. The short trip to school—down the road, on the bus or in the car—is a journey over a mountain to a child. A journey into their own other world, where we may guard over them from a distance but not intrude. A world where they can learn to live without us, if only for a few hours at a time.

trust

Trust is one of the greatest compliments we can pay our children.

Their sense of pride and achievement
is swelled when they hear us say,
"I don't need to watch, I know you'll
do it properly," or, "If I lend you some
money, you'll have to remember to pay
it back because I may forget." It shows
them that we believe in them.

Let not the sun go down
upon your wrath.

No matter what our children have done during the day, and how angry we may have been with them, bedtime is a time to wipe the slate clean so that they can sleep peacefully and start the next day afresh. However disobedient they may be, we still love them, and bedtime is the time to remind them of it. Then they can drift off to sleep, warm and soft and comforted, knowing that they are safe in our love no matter what they do.

bedtime

friends

The old oak and the young sapling grow side by side.

When we look around at other mothers who have good relationships with grown up children, those relationships are always built on solid friendships. Whatever other dynamics are at play, mother and child are firm friends and enjoy each other's company. It is never too early to make a friend of our children, to enjoy their company for its own sake, to share jokes with them, and go out together simply for the pleasure of being together.

As it sits on its branch, the owl listens intently for the sound of its prey scuttling through the undergrowth. How often do we listen this closely to our child? Too often we finish the sentence they are carefully trying to piece together, or reply with a distracted, "Really, darling? That's nice." Sometimes we take their words at face value when they are masking a worry or a fear, because we aren't really listening to them. And yet our child deserves for us to listen as intently as the owl, for every nuance of what they tell us.

listening

praise

Even flowers grow better when they are encouraged.

A child only really knows it has done well when we tell it so. And if we want good behavior from our child, we should be willing to pay for it in praise. And that means praising not only active achievements but also passive ones—praising our child for not misbehaving. A bedtime "You've been good all day today. Well done!" shows them that we noticed, that it was worth the effort. Praise for a child is like water and sunshine to a flower, helping it grow bigger and brighter and happier.

independence

The lark rises from sullen earth into the sky, singing ever more sweetly as it climbs. A child starts out feeling it is a mere extension of us, and as it grows it slowly breaks free and rises toward its own sky. The more independent it becomes, the more it starts to sing its own song. And when we see it high above our head, singing a song we never taught it, then we know we have given it the freedom it deserves.

The mother hen keeps her
chicks safe from dangers she learned to
recognize when she herself was a chick.

past childhood

If we cannot remember our own childhood, we cannot help our children through theirs. We need to search our memories to understand how our children feel when they are upset or angry, over-excited or confused. Only then can we truly empathize, and recognize when they need firmness and when they need sympathy.

laughter

Laugh and the world
laughs with you.

If we could choose one quality for our children, it would be happiness. And the ability to laugh is one of the most valuable talents for bringing happiness. We can help our children learn to laugh by sharing laughter with them as often as possible, by letting them see us laugh at words and actions, thoughts and pictures. We can teach them to find humor even in misfortune, so that for the rest of their lives they need never be without laughter.

example

A young foal follows its mother around the field, copying her as she walks, feeds, and sleeps.

Our children learn from us; our example sets the pattern for them. If we talk over them when we speak, or interrupt them, they will do the same. If we shout when we are angry, so will they. If we tell them what to do instead of asking them politely, they will copy us. If our children have qualities we dislike, we should question ourselves as to where they learned them from.

not us

We insult our children if we deny them their own identity. Just because we were talented at reading at their age, or we enjoy classical music, or we have an aptitude for sport, it doesn't mean they will. We may always have been even tempered, or confident with strangers, but our children are allowed to be different. More than that; we can enjoy the differences.

Even if you graft a rose from another rose, its stems will not grow into the same exact shape as its parent plant.

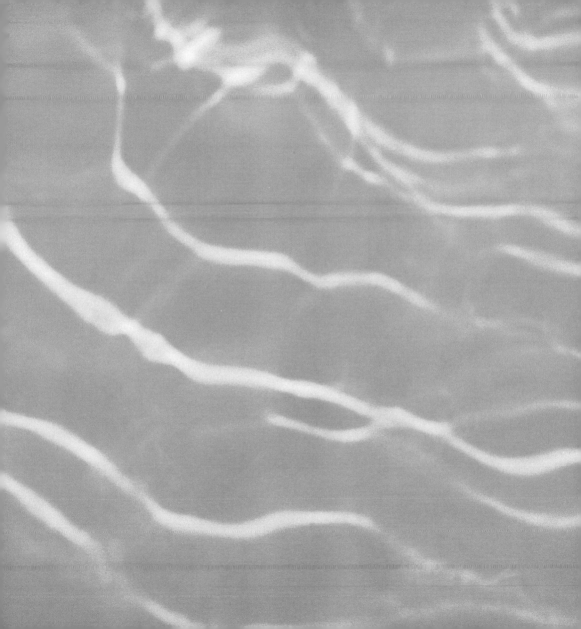

respect

The surest way to teach a child respect for others is to treat it with respect itself. Too many mothers speak sharply to their children without need, or show no consideration for their child's toys, or expect them to abandon a favorite game without any warning. We should treat our children as we would treat our best friends—they should be our best friends—at least while they are being friendly and cooperative in return.

boundaries

If you put a lamb in a field which has no fences it will wander and become lost, and it will be prey to all sorts of dangers. If you surround the field with a fence which breaks as soon as the lamb leans on it, it will still wander. But if you build a strong fence, the lamb will be safe and it will know it is safe. It will know that you built the fence because you cared for its welfare, not because you wanted to shut it in. If the field is fenced to the right size, neither too cramped nor too large, the lamb will enjoy its freedom fully within its boundaries.

labels

If you tell a child they are bad, and treat them as if they were bad, they will behave badly to fulfill your expectation of them.

Children are vulnerable and suggestible, and we need only say, "You are stupid," for them to believe it. We are careful as mothers to give our children only positive labels. Our child is not stupid, even if the thing it has done was stupid. Even after a disobedient act, our child is still a good child who has done a naughty thing, and not a naughty child.

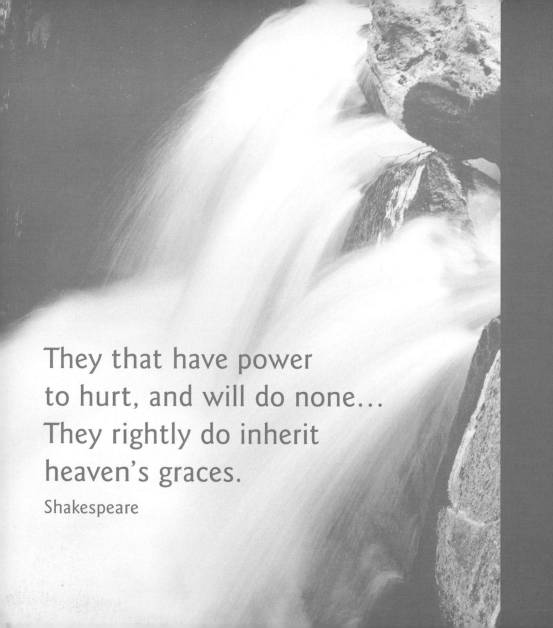

They that have power
to hurt, and will do none…
They rightly do inherit
heaven's graces.

Shakespeare

As a mother, we wield a terrifying power over our child. We can influence the rest of its life more deeply than almost anything else ever will. Our behavior, over the first sixteen years of our child's life, will determine much of their future happiness, their ability to form relationships, their confidence, their skill as a parent, their freedom to choose the career they want, their pleasures and their dislikes. We can never forget the depth of our responsibility toward them.

discipline

A fruit bush which is left to grow as it pleases becomes leggy and ragged and bears little fruit. But a fruit bush which is pruned and trained reaches its full potential and bears armfuls of fruit.

We do not discipline our
children to punish them for
punishment's sake, or to save them
from irritating or inconveniencing us.
We discipline them so that in time they can
grow into the best shape to bear prolific fruit.

be anything

Who would believe that an ugly duckling could grow up to be a beautiful swan?

Or that a tiny shoot, barely visible above the ground, could eventually become a tall, strong tree?

We set our children's horizons for them, and they do not think to question them until it is too late. If we tell them they will never be more than a scraggy duck or a little sapling, they will believe us, and that is all they will become. But if we tell them they can be an elegant swan or the tallest tree in the wood, we open up their horizons so that they can be whatever they want.

adventure

A mother was waiting on a station platform with her little son. The train was late, and gradually the platform began to fill up. It became ever more crowded as they waited, and they grew bored and tired. Eventually, the platform was so full that people began to jostle and push. The train finally came in, but there were so many people that many of them couldn't get on, including the mother and her son. As the train pulled out, the little boy was starting to become nervous, worried, and intimidated. His mother knelt down beside him on the platform, and smiled at him.

"This," she said, "is what they call an adventure."

spoiling

The bonsai tree demands care and time, food and water, the best pot to grow in and the best surroundings to show it off. We all want to give our child the things which they will enjoy and which will stimulate them. And if we can afford to buy them a new bike or take them abroad on holiday, so we should. That is not how children get spoiled. It is giving children their own way, giving in to them, letting them feel that they control us rather than the other way around, which spoils them. Only by letting the bonsai grow as it chooses, without keeping it under control, do we spoil and ruin it.

gratitude

The sunflower does not thank the sun for shining on it, even though it could not grow without it.

If we expect thanks from our children for mothering them well, we will be disappointed. Why should they thank us? We only do the job we ourselves volunteered for. And it is an important job for which the standards are therefore high—we have to shine simply to avoid failing. Our children may thank us one day—or they may not. But as soon as we expect thanks, we cease to deserve them.

education

We send our children to school to educate them, and yet school is such a tiny part of their education.

School is important, but it is nothing to the education we can offer our child. We can give our child the individual attention that a school cannot, and build on interests and talents with books and videos, visits and museum trips, and most of all by talking to them. Telling them what we know, and allowing them to impress us with what they can tell us. Unlike school, we can help them to become experts, with a greater knowledge than everyone else.

sand in the hair

As a young child you can lie on the sand
as the waves wash around you, and not
even think of the trouble you will have
later getting the sand out of your hair.

You can splash in the mud and forget that you will have to have a bath later. Such total enjoyment is hard as an adult, because we look ahead, and see the trouble we are storing up for ourselves. Once our children lose this ability to be wholeheartedly absorbed, they will never be able to reclaim it. We can only help them to preserve such enjoyment for as long as possible.

rivers

The smallest trickle
turns into a
stream; the
stream tumbles
into the river.
The river broadens
and deepens
until it becomes
a wide estuary.
And at last it
flows out into
the sea, and then
who knows where?

Our children start as small bundles of simple thoughts and desires—food, sleep and comfort. As they grow, their feelings become deeper and more complex, they develop new ideas and interests, they acquire knowledge and understanding. And at last, they are ready to pour themselves out of the little world we have created for them at home, and into the world of the unknown. And then who knows where?

In times of drought, the river may run dry. But it is only a matter of time before the rain will fall and the streams and rivers will flow again.

dry river

As a mother, we sometimes feel we have been drained dry emotionally, and have no more to give our children. But if we wait just a little, and spoil ourselves as much as we can with a relaxing bath or an early night, it won't be long before our emotional well fills up again and we are refreshed.

There are millions of stars in the sky, and
although each one is beautiful, it is the
effect of seeing millions of them twinkling
together which really takes the breath away.

Each of our children is made up
of millions of little
characteristics, quirks, and
qualities, but what makes them
truly unique and wonderful is
the combination of all those
traits making up a whole person.
We may be tempted to wish
away some of the more
frustrating or difficult qualities,
but to do that would alter the
balance of the whole.

stars

Sourcebooks, Inc.
P.O. Box 4410, Naperville, Illinois 60567-4410
(630) 961-3900
FAX: (630) 961-2168

Text © Roni Jay 2000
Cover design: The Big Idea
Interior design: Bet Ayer
Cover image: Mike Bentley, Flowers & Foliage
Interior images: © Digital Vision
Series Editor: Elizabeth Carr

Printed in Italy

MQ 10 9 8 7 6 5 4 3 2 1

ISBN: 1-57071-643-9

Note on the CD

The music that accompanies this book has been specially commissioned from composer David Baird. Trained in music and drama in Wales, and on the staff of the Welsh National Opera & Drama company, David has composed many soundtracks for both the theater and radio.

The CD can be played quietly through headphones while relaxing or meditating on the text. Alternatively, lie on the floor between two speakers placed at equal distances from you. Try and center your thoughts, and allow the soundtrack to wash over you and strip away the distracting layers of the outside world.